Written by JENNIFER SHARPE • Illustrated by

The MASS and the Manger

My Interactive Christmas Story

ASCENSION
Kids

Twinkling lights, manger scene,
midnight Mass—what could it mean?
Christmas Eve is here!

Mary, Joseph, baby so small.
Shepherds and wise men follow God's call.
That first Christmas, long ago,
not so different from now, you know!
Jesus comes to us still now.
Lift each page, and
you'll see how.

The Spirit leads the way this night.
The holy couple bathed in light—
with Christmas in their hearts!

And now a holy path I take.
A joyful journey I will make.

Like Mother Mary long ago,
and Joseph too, I want to go—
to meet the newborn King.

Joseph has looked everywhere.
No one has the room to spare,
but one man lets them in.

Above their heads a star is placed.
It draws men near to see your face.
You make their hearts brand-new.

Mary—late that night in prayer—
knows that you will soon be there,
God made flesh for us.

But look! It's time! The angels sing!
And through the night, their voices ring!
The shepherds rush to see.

Your mother hugs you as you rest.
With all her heart, she loves you best—
her Savior and her Lord.

Little baby who brings us grace,
Joseph gazes upon your face
and gives his heart to you.

The Magi from the East came near
because they saw the star appear—
a sign of something new.

The wise men brought their gifts to you,
and as they gave them, their hearts grew
to love you more and more.

King Herod wished the baby ill,
but Joseph's dream revealed God's will—
to Egypt they must flee.

In accordance with CIC 827, permission to publish has been granted on
May 25, 2023, by the Most Reverend Mark S. Rivituso, Auxiliary Bishop,
Archdiocese of St. Louis. Permission to publish is an indication that nothing contrary
to Church teaching is contained in this particular work. It does not imply any
endorsement of the opinions expressed in the publication, or a general
endorsement of any author; nor is any liability assumed by this permission.

Ascension
PO Box 1990
West Chester, PA 19380
1-800-376-0520
ascensionpress.com

Cover design: Giulia Fini

Printed in China
23 24 25 26 27 5 4 3 2 1

ISBN 978-1-954882-08-9